*For Diane*

Copyright © 1989 Paula Cloonan
First published 1989 by Blackie and Son Ltd

British Library Cataloguing in Publication Data

Moore, Clement Clark
  The night before Christmas
  1. English language.   Readers—For
schools
I. Title      II.  Cloonan, Paula
428.6

  ISBN 0-216-92721-8


First American edition published in 1989 by
Peter Bedrick Books
2112 Broadway, Rm. 318
New York, NY 10023

Library of Congress Cataloging-in-Publication Data
Moore, Clement Clark, 1779–1863.
    The night before Christmas/Clement Clark  Moore; illustrated by
Paula Cloonan.
      p.    cm.
    Summary: A well-known poem about an important Christmas visitor.
    ISBN 0-87226-416-5
    1. Santa Claus—Juvenile poetry.   2.  Christmas—Juvenile poetry.
    3. Children's poetry, American.  [1. Santa Claus—Poetry.
    2. Christmas—Poetry.   3. American poetry.   4. Narrative poetry.]
    I. Cloonan, Paula, ill.   II. Title.
    PS2429.M5N5   1989c
    811'.2——dc20                                      89-6560 CIP AC


Blackie and Son Ltd
7 Leicester Place
London WC2H 7BP

Printed in Spain by
  Salingraf, S.A.L.

# ·THE NIGHT BEFORE· CHRISTMAS

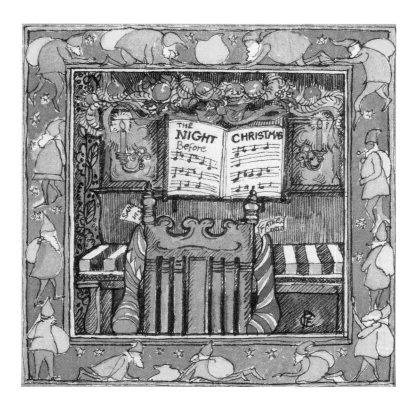

## Clement C Moore and Paula Cloonan

**Blackie**
**London**

**Bedrick/Blackie**
**New York**

'Twas the night before Christmas,
   when all through the house
Not a creature was stirring,
   not even a mouse.
The stockings were hung
   by the chimney with care,
In hopes that Saint Nicholas
   soon would be there.

The children were nestled
all snug in their beds,
While visions of sugarplums
danced in their heads.

And Mama in her kerchief
   and I in my cap,
Had just settled our brains
   for a long winter's nap,
When out on the lawn
   there arose such a clatter,
I sprang from my bed
   to see what was the matter.
Away to the window
   I flew like a flash,
Tore open the shutters,
   and threw up the sash.

The moon, on the breast
  of the new-fallen snow,
Gave the lustre of midday
  to objects below.
When, what to my wondering
  eyes should appear . . .

But a miniature sleigh,
    and eight tiny reindeer!
With a little old driver,
    so lively and quick
I knew in a moment
    it must be Saint Nick!

More rapid than eagles
　　his coursers they came,
And whistled, and shouted,
　　and called them by name.
'Now, Dasher! Now, Dancer!
　　Now, Prancer and Vixen!
On, Comet! On, Cupid!
　　On, Donder and Blitzen!
To the top of the porch,
　　to the top of the wall!
Now, dash away, dash away,
　　dash away all!'

As dry leaves that before
the wild hurricane fly
When they meet with an obstacle
mount to the sky;
So up to the housetop
the coursers they flew,
With a sleigh full of toys,
and Saint Nicholas too.

And then, in a twinkling,
   I heard on the roof
The prancing and pawing
   of each little hoof.
As I drew in my head
   and was turning around,
Down the chimney Saint Nicholas
   came with a bound.

He was dressed all in fur
from his head to his foot,
And his clothes were all
tarnished with ashes and soot;
A bundle of toys
he had flung on his back,
And he looked like a pedlar
just opening his pack.

His eyes, how they twinkled!
   His dimples, how merry!
His cheeks were like roses,
   his nose like a cherry;
His droll little mouth
   was drawn up like a bow,
And the beard on his chin
   was as white as the snow.
The stump of a pipe
   he held tight in his teeth,
And the smoke, it encircled
   his head like a wreath;
He had a broad face
   and a little round belly
That shook, when he laughed
   like a bowlful of jelly!

He was chubby and plump—
   a right jolly old elf;
And I laughed when I saw him,
   in spite of myself.
A wink of his eye,
   and a twist of his head,
Soon gave me to know
   I had nothing to dread.
He spoke not a word,
   but went straight to his work,
And filled all the stockings;
   then turned with a jerk,

And laying his finger
aside of his nose,
And giving a nod,
up the chimney he rose.

He sprang to his sleigh,
   to his team gave a whistle,
And away they all flew
   like the down of a thistle;
But I heard him exclaim,
   'ere he drove out of sight:
'Happy Christmas to all,
   and to all a good night!'